Freedom

by Lucile McIntyre

Baker's Plays
7611 Sunset Blvd.
Los Angeles, CA 90042
bakersplays.com

NOTICE

This book is offered for sale at the price quoted only on the understanding that, if any additional copies of the whole or any part are necessary for its production, such additional copies will be purchased. The attention of all purchasers is directed to the following: This work is protected under the copyright laws of the United States of America, in the British Empire, including the Dominion of Canada, and all other countries adhering to the Universal Copyright Convention. Violations of the Copyright Law are punishable by fine or imprisonment, or both. The copying or duplication of this work or any part of this work, by hand or by any process, is an infringement of the copyright and will be vigorously prosecuted.

This play may not be produced by amateurs or professionals for public or private performance without first submitting application for performing rights. Royalties are due on all performances whether for charity or gain, or whether admission is charged or not Since performance of this play without the payment of the royalty fee renders anybody participating liable to severe penalties imposed by the law, anybody acting in this play should be sure, before doing so, that the royalty fee has been paid. Professional rights, reading rights, radio broadcasting, television and all mechanical rights, etc. are strictly reserved. Application for performing rights should be made directly to BAKER'S PLAYS.

No one shall commit or authorize any act or omission by which the copyright of, or the right to copyright, this play may be impaired. No one shall make any changes in this play for the purpose of production.

Publication of this play does not imply availability for performance. Both amateurs and professionals considering a production are strongly advised in their own interest to apply to Baker's Plays for written permission before starting rehearsals, advertising, or booking a theatre.

Whenever the play is produced, the author's name must be carried in all publicity, advertising and programs. Also, the following notice must appear on all printed programs, "Produced by special arrangement with Baker's Plays."

Licensing fees for *FREEDOM FIRES* is based on a per performance rate and payable one week in advance of the production.

Please consult the Baker's Plays website at www.bakersplays.com or our current print catalogue for up to date licensing fee information.

FREEDOM FIRES
ISBN 978-0-87440-193-6
#1848-B

CHARACTERS

LYNN MCKENZIE . . . . .American soldier, Iraqi War

JESSIE FINLEY . . . . .American soldier, Iraqi War

RICHARD KRAMER. . . . . .American soldier, Viet Nam War

PEARL CAGNEY .American soldier, World War II

DAVID CARPENTER .American soldier, Civil War

EZEKIAL SLOCUMB . . . . .American soldier, Revolutionary War

VOICE . . . . God

MEDIC. . . . . .American soldier, Iraqi War

RESCUE TEAM . . . . .American soldier, Iraqi War

(As many as desired.)

PLACE

IRAQ

TIME

2006

PRODUCTION NOTES

SETTING: The desert at night can be portrayed with a bare stage. If desired, small levels may be used to give illusions of piles of sand. The dream window can be a platform enclosed by drapes or screens or a scrim. This should be several feet high so that the audience sees the dream images looking down upon the injured soldier. This dream window is li t only when the soldier of the moment is speaking.

COSTUMES: Military fatigues are used for the soldiers in the Iraqi War. Each soldier of the dream window should be dressed in the period he represents . Stay away from new and fresh looks for Ezekial and David.

LIGHTING: Sensitive lighting actually creates the desired effect of the desert at night. The lighting on the dream window fades in and out slowly to reveal the hero .

SOUND: The sound effects that can enrich the performance may range from rounds of machine guns firing , distant single shots, explosions, voices from the distant side of the battlefield, trucks cranking, etc. Sound effects can be another character here.

PROPS: Props will be military related for the American soldiers. They will carry military weapons, canteens, typical supplies, etc. Each hero in the dream window will have unique props for his time period. (For example, Pearl will have bed sheet lengths of white cotton strips which she is rolling for bandages.)

This play is dedicated to every American Soldier who has valued your freedom and mine more than life itself.

(**SCENE:** *Two female soldiers dressed in field uniforms scramble across the stage. One almost drags the other in front of a sand ridge. The healthy one is terrified.*)

LYNN. (**LYNN** *pulls her injured comrade with determination.*) Come on, Jesse, breathe…just a little further.

(**LYNN** *helps* **JESSE** *to sit down in front of what appears to be a sand ridge.*)

I think we're out of sight up here.

JESSE. How did he see me, Lynn? I was under the hummer. I know I shot him first! *(She is overcome by pain.)*

LYNN. Hush! Be still. Don't talk now!

JESSE. I don't believe this. I marched in a protest against firearms once.

(She grabs the stronger soldier by the collar and tries to convince her of her intentions.)

I never wanted to be in a real war. I just wanted to learn how to take down bullies.

LYNN. I just wanted to get fast enough to get away from bullies.

JESSE. Lynn, my arm hurts. Kick me in the leg to get my mind off the pain.

LYNN. Forget it. I'm not going to kick you. You don't need to move right now.

JESSE. I can't die here Lynn. *(Wracked by pain.)* My dad would never forgive me. He never believed I could be a soldier. *(Shaking and trembling.)*

LYNN. Be quiet! *(She throws her own jacket over* **JESSE** *to comfort her.)* Save your energy. We have to stop this bleeding. (**LYNN** *tries to tie off the arm to stop the blood.*)

(Stage lights cross fade as a dream window above stage level lights up to reveal a U.S. soldier from the Vietnam War.)

RICHARD. *(Looking down on the two soldiers.)* Hey Jess! The scenery there in Iraq is different than it was for me in Vietnam. Yet, you are in the same place I was once. This is the moment you decide to live or die.

JESSE. *(Fitfully from the dark below.)* Who are you? *(Hesitating a moment.)* I said, who are you?

RICHARD. Kramer, Richard Kramer. Green Barrett, Fort Bragg, North Carolina. The last place I wanted to be was Vietnam where I thought Satan was after me for certain because the jungles of Vietnam were full of snakes. I went into service to fight for all of my ancestors who died at Auschwitz. My grandmother was 4'10" so the Nazis didn't think she was of any use to them for work. She and four of her five children were marched into what they thought was a community shower. Without warning, she and the four children were gassed to death because they were Jews. My grandfather had already been killed when he tried to pull my grandmother away from the soldiers who were loading the women and children on the train. The soldier shot him in the face right there in front of his wife and children. My father was the only member of his family to survive. He was eleven at the time and big for his age. The Nazis thought he would be useful for digging the mass graves where thousands of Jews were dumped on top of each other for all of eternity. My dad survived the torture and starvation and risked his life hiding away on a ship to come to America. He always vowed that he would never allow another Auschwitz as long as he lived. So, the defense of freedom was engrained in me every day of my life. None of our training could have adequately prepared our company for a battlefield where we couldn't see three feet in front of us for vines and bushes. Oh, we had done all the right things just as we had been trained.

We were confident and ready. We were the elite fighters, the Green Barrett. No Viet Cong was going to get by us. On a night like this, we were doing recon by a little village. Jesse, I was put down by what I thought was a kid. I saw him before he saw me, but things didn't register. The grenade he tossed took out anything in its path, wiping off my left leg and another soldier's chances to see again, before I could lift my gun. Two soldiers behind me never moved again. Our fifth man was scattered over various trees and vines. It was that quick. Part of me wanted to stay in the jungle and die right there, but then I saw that young kid knifed to death by a superior because he couldn't kill all five of us. That twelve year-old boy had no choice to fight or not to fight. At that moment the fire in my soul replaced the pain in my leg. You see Jesse, in communism there's no freedom of choice. Tell me, soldier. Would a woman in Iraq have the freedom to do what you could do back in Wilmington? That's a laugh isn't it? You have a decision to make officer. Make it now Jesse.

(Lights cross fade.)

JESSE. *(From the dim light on stage.)* Wait! Wait! I need to ask you something.

LYNN. I'm right here. You're hallucinating. Try not to move.

JESSE. I have to teach my little sister how to do fast pitch. She wants to play next year. I have her lifting weights until I go back on leave. She has my whole 3 weeks planned. *(Suddenly she becomes aware.)* My arm is numb. *(Becoming hysterical)* I don't feel my hand. Lynn, I don't feel my hand.

(With her good hand, **JESSE** *grabs* **LYNN**'s *collar to express her sense of urgency.)*

LYNN. Be quiet, Jess. *(Trying to hold her down.)* Help will be here soon.

(Dream window lights up above stage to reveal a World War II nurse in full attire of the time.)

PEARL. Get up girl! You still have a job to do. *(Her tough* *manner is projected in a hoarse whisper at first.)* Night time is your safest time to move. *(Giving reassurance.)* The enemy ran like scalded cats after that round you fired from under your truck. You're a cagey little thing. None of their men expected you. They only saw the truck driver. You took 'em down girl.

JESSE. *(Trying to lift head.)* Do I know you?

*(**PEARL** is rolling bandages made from dingy white bed sheets. Some strips are thrown loosely over her shoulder.)*

PEARL. Oh, no, you just read about me during high school when you did that study on U.S. women in the military, for Mr. Ross. He gave you a "B", remember. You took him on! *(Laughing to herself.)* He finally gave you an "A."

JESSE. *(Smiling to herself.)* Yeah...He was never in the military, but he was certain that women didn't belong in any part of it.

PEARL. You can't let all of us down, Jesse. We nurses even took a lot of junk from our own guys at times. Believe me, they wouldn't have made it without us. Ask any soldier who was lucky enough to get to sick bay. I've cupped more than a few necks to force the blood back through a man's body. I've crammed my hand into mutilated flesh to pull a shattered femoral artery back out in order to clamp it off to keep a soldier from bleeding to death. In World War II, medicine and first aid were less than advanced. You actually have it pretty good where first aid is concerned. Listen girl, you don't want me to come down there and pinch off that artery. Anyway, if you fold now, you've wasted four years of college and some other softball star might as well have used that four year scholarship you put in your hip pocket. So, why don't you show me what you got, Missy, or have you already given up?!?

JESSE. *(Struggling to sit up.)* I'm not giving up! I can still fight. *(Forcing herself to stand.)* We have to get back to one of the trucks. *(Bleary eyed.)* I can get there by myself.

(JESSE collapses, struggling in frustration with raw wounds in sand. LYNN knows she cannot delay any longer and pushes JESSE back down by the sand ridge as she departs.)

LYNN. Wait here, Jesse. I'll be right back...hang on.

(She runs in the direction they had been moving.)

(Dream window lights up, revealing a Civil War soldier)

DAVID. Miss Jesse, I feel for you. It's mighty hard to fall to enemy fire.

JESSE. Who's that? I said who's that?

DAVID. David, David Carpenter, Ma'am. I never dreamed I'd be raising a weapon to kill another human being. I left home out of pride. I thought I had to join the other men from Rocky Point. When we finally got to the clearing where the battle broke out, I raised my gun like everyone else. Just as I pulled the trigger, I recognized my own little brother's face as my gun's fire took him by surprise. The last time I had seen him had been when he had the big fight with the men from our church, over the slavery issue. He ran away that very night. He was fourteen, fourteen years old. His big innocent eyes had stared at me in the kitchen that night as he said, "What about you, David? What do you stand for?" I showed my true colors, those of a coward. I felt my father's eyes, the parson's eyes, and the eyes of every man in that room. I could not meet the eyes of my little brother. As the museums have since recounted for children of the future, brother fought brother for the sake of freedom. When the truth set in, I threw down my gun and raced to my brother's side. I scooped him up in my arms where his last words were "Think, David. Understand what it is that you stand for." So, what is it that you stand for, Miss Jesse?

(The light on the dream window fades as stage lights come up. LYNN enters with a MEDIC.)

LYNN. *(To the* **MEDIC** *with her:)* Over here. *(To* **JESSE***:)* Jesse! Time to shine. Help is here.

*(***LYNN** *and one or two other soldiers rush to attend to* **JESSE***'s wounds. Wasting no time, the* **MEDIC** *works on the arm and* **LYNN** *applies a disinfectant from the medic's bag. They get* **JESSE** *to drink water from the* **MEDIC***'s canteen.)*

MEDIC. DRINK!

(They hook her up to an IV and administer other first aid.)

BP is 50 over 30. Come on Lieutenant.

LYNN. Jesse, this is not a good time to die. You pray, you hear me?

(Dream window lights up to reveal man of the 1770's dressed in ragged farm attire of the time. Stage lights fade.)

*(***EZEKIAL** *may carry a makeshift gun or long stick which could have been a fighting instrument.)*

EZEKIAL SLOCUMB. So, your name's Jesse, huh? My name's Slocumb, Ezekial Slocumb. I'm no stranger to the sight of blood, Miss Jesse.

JESSE. Where are you? I can't see you.

EZEKIAL. I worked my first twelve years in North Carolina for a wealthy Englishman to pay him back for bringing my family and me over here to America. I'm what some people call an indentured servant. In February of 1775, I joined a few other fellows from the backwoods of North Carolina in a little "swimming party" over at Moore's Creek in Pender County. You see, we got wind of the fact that 1600 highlanders were joining the revolutionary leader, Col. Donald McDonald to take over our port down in Charleston, SC. This was serious news to those of us living off the land. Well, we only pulled together a thousand men...but one of our thousand men was worth ten of anybody else's. You know what we did? *(He is most amused with* *his rebel shenanigans.)* The night before we heard they were coming through we crept around in the dark at the bridge and removed most of the planks from the stringers of the bridge. Then, we slathered those two long poles crossing that river, with two buckets of lard that Henry Michaels had brought from his January hog killings down in Brunswick County. As the Tories came upon the creek sight, all they noticed was empty entrenchments. We were all nested down on the other side of the creek. Well, the old Col. McDonald had become sick and couldn't carry on with his battle plans. However, his two young upstart assistants were raring to be heroes. It seems that they talked the Col. into letting them carry on in his place. Now mind you, anyone getting from point "A" to point "B" had to go over, under, or through Moore's Creek. So, ladies and gentlemen, on one of the greased stringers pranced the dapper Captain John Campbell and on the other stringer, danced the very refined Lt. Col McLeod. We didn't make a move 'till they were right in front of us. Their men came running behind them, brand new tricorn hats a'bouncing and broadswords a'gleaming in the moonlight. We then opened up our two cannons and the few muskets that had been scraped together, like the whole world depended on the few of us boys crouched down there in our ragged farm clothes. Moore's Creek water was red with redcoats. We only lost two men in the whole skirmish. We showed 'em. We were like David and they were like Goliath. When the first charge of men either drowned or succumbed to their powder wounds, the well dressed men left on the bank ran for their lives back to where they came from. From that morning on, the world knew that we Americans were into freedom for the long haul. We were never again going to be oppressed by any country who showed no concern for our individual rights and freedoms. The next month, Patrick Henry spoke for all of us when he told the President and the House "Forbid it, Almighty God! I know not what course others may take; but as for me, give me liberty or give me death."

(Dream window lights fade. Dim lights come up on stage revealing the same picture as before.)

*(During the next sequence, **JESSE** converses with God, who comes to her as a **VOICE**.)*

JESSE. *(In great distress and fitfulness.)* Dear Lord…

VOICE. YES, MY CHILD.

(God is not seen.)

JESSE. Help me. *(Voice fades weakly.)*

VOICE. TAKE MY HAND…LOOK UPON MY FACE.

JESSE. I can't move…I feel numb.

VOICE. JESSE FINLEY, YOU ARE A CHILD OF GOD! LEAN ON ME.

JESSE. Lord? Where have you been?

(She begins to rise in slow motion as all others are still.)

VOICE. I HAVE NEVER LEFT YOU. I HAVE PRESERVED YOUR LIFE MANY TIMES IN ORDER TO BRING YOU HERE TONIGHT.

JESSE. Forgive my sense of humor, Lord, but being gunned down in Iraq was not one of my long term goals.

VOICE. STAND…STAND UP AND LOOK AROUND. YOUR COMPANY, UNDER YOUR COMMAND, TOOK OUT AN OPERATION OF BULLIES.

JESSE. *(Attempting to stand.)* Lord, bullies are people who take advantage of anyone they can overpower, like the kids who picked on Tom Chisum, always breaking his glasses, just because he was smart…you know…in fourth grade?

*(**JESSE**'s rescuers do not see her moving around as she talks to God but see only the soldier on the stretcher.)*

VOICE. REMEMBER THAT YOU SOLVED THAT BULLY-ING PROBLEM WHEN YOU TOLD THEM THEY'D HAVE TO COME THROUGH YOU TO BREAK

TOM'S GLASSES?

JESSE. You saw that? The fire inside me just took over. I thought I was going to the principal's office for the first time in my life. That crowd said I was trying to pick a fight.

VOICE. BUT...THE BULLIES BACKED OFF. SOMETIMES ONE VOICE IS ALL THAT IS NEEDED TO PRE-SERVE FREEDOM.

JESSE. Lord, this is not fourth grade. I'm in a different ball-game now.

VOICE. THESE BULLIES ALLOW NO EDUCATION FOR FEMALES LIKE YOU!

JESSE. But, Lord, some of the women here have been edu-cated. One of our translators is proof of that. She is so smart.

VOICE. AT GREAT COST, JESSE. THE PARENTS OF YOUR TRANSLATOR WERE CANNED TO DEATH IN THE TOWN SQUARE WHEN SADAM HEARD THAT THEY HAD TAUGHT A FEMALE CHILD IN THEIR HOME. SHE HELPS YOU AS A WAY TO HONOR HER PARENTS.

JESSE. Oh...I never knew that.

VOICE. THERE IS NO CHOICE OF LIFE MATES HERE, EITHER. SUICIDE IS COMMON. MANY YOUNG GIRLS DO NOT WANT TO BE MARRIED TO OLDER RICH MEN SELECTED BY THEIR PARENTS.

JESSE. I know I'd prefer selecting my breakfast partner.

VOICE. AND NO CHOICE OF THE GOD A PERSON WILL SERVE.

JESSE. I would at least want to choose my own time to pray.

VOICE. AND ANOTHER MATTER OF INTEREST, NO VOICE OR VOTE IN WHO GOVERNS ONE'S PEOPLE OR WHAT GOVERNMENT IS FOLLOWED.

JESSE. That does it Lord. I feel the fire. I have to fight! But, *(Looking into the faces of the soldiers working on the space where her body lay earlier.)* I may not be well enough now.

Our medic looks so serious.

VOICE. DID YOU FORGET? I'M STILL IN CHARGE. I WOULD NOT HAVE MOLDED YOU EVERY DAY OF YOUR LIFE IF THIS MOMENT HAD NOT BEEN IN MY PLAN.

JESSE. Wait…if you planned everything…what was the deal with Allen Murphy standing me up for the senior prom?

VOICE. I WANTED YOU TO KNOW THAT ALL THINGS WOULD NOT ALWAYS GO AS YOU PLANNED.

JESSE. Oh…I suppose you knew I might have this little setback over here tonight.

VOICE. NOW, YOU'RE THINKING. SO, GET BACK ON THAT STRETCHER AND LET MY PEOPLE HELP YOU, FOR I HAVE ALLOWED THEM TO LEARN HOW TO BRING HEALING TO THEIR FELLOW MAN.

(Upbeat, smiling, and energized, JESSE salutes what we assume she sees as The Face Of God, above the center of the audience, on the back row…)

JESSE. Yes, Sir!

(She lies down on the stretcher. The other soldiers remain intent upon the wounded soldier they see on the stretcher.)

MEDIC. *(Manually opening and looking into JESSE's eyes.)* Her pupils are good.

LYNN. She's in there all right.

MEDIC. Her blood pressure is up. Let's get her out of here.

(LYNN, another soldier and a MEDIC rush their precious cargo away for transport.)

LYNN. This lieutenant is gonna' rumble tonight!

MEDIC. Keep that bag elevated so it will flow. Blood does wonders!

(They carry her off the battlefield.)

End of Play